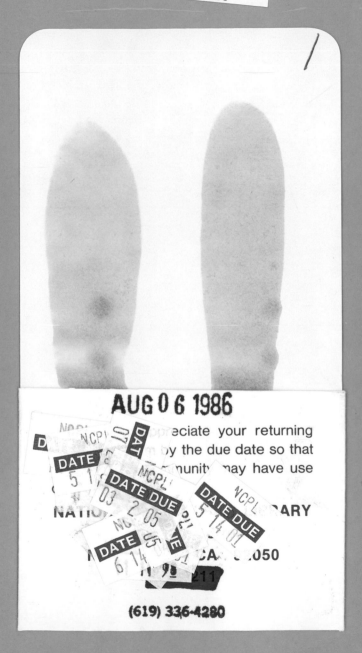

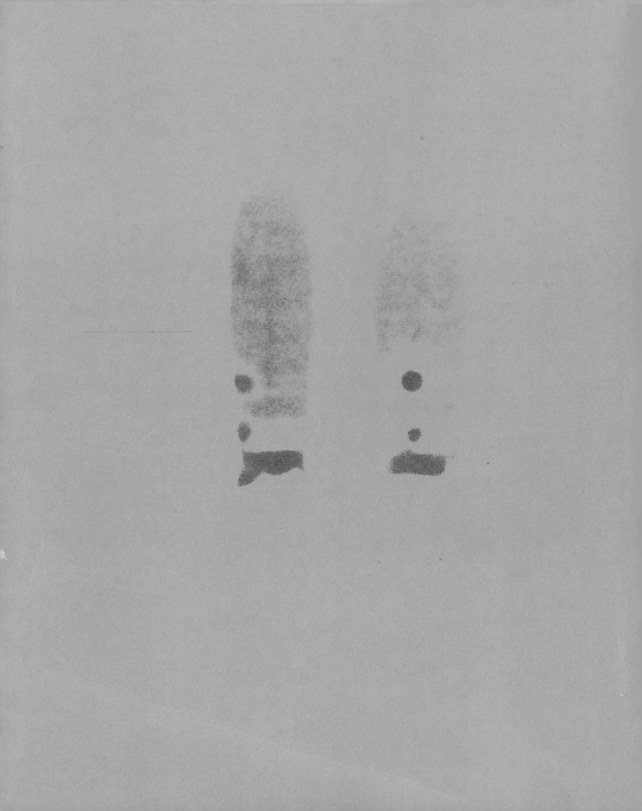

ETHIOPIA

IRENE CUMMING KLEEBERG

ETHIOPIA

Franklin Watts
New York/London/Toronto/Sydney/1986
A First Book

Map by Vantage Art, Inc.

Photographs courtesy of:
CARE: opp. p. 1, p. 54;
United Nations: pp. 4, 6;
Magnum Photos: pp. 8, 15, 17, 26, 40, 48;
UPI/Bettmann Newsphotos: pp. 10, 29, 30, 36;
The Bettmann Archive: p. 22;
New York Public Library Picture Collection: p. 44.

Library of Congress Cataloging in Publication Data
Kleeberg, Irene Cumming.
Ethiopia.
(A First book)
Bibliography: p.
Includes index.
Summary: Surveys the history, religion, language,
and current political, economic, and social problems
of this country of contradictions.
1. Ethiopia—Juvenile literature. [1. Ethiopia]
I. Title.
DT373.K54   1986   963 916.3 85-26616
ISBN 0-531-10115-0

CONTENTS

ETHIOPIA

CHAPTER 1

IN THE NEWS

The country of Ethiopia is in the news almost every day. And almost all the news is tragic. It is about children who will never grow up, about starvation, about the lack of water, and about how the desert is taking over more and more land. The news is about war and about food sent to the needy that never reaches them.

One of the greatest tragedies is that Ethiopia wasn't always like this. Not very long ago, life for the people of Ethiopia was getting better. Education was slowly spreading throughout the country, and some positive changes were made in the government.

About 90 percent of the people farmed or raised cattle or sheep and there was enough rain, except in the desert and semi-desert areas. The rain meant that the people could grow food for themselves and their families and still have some left over to sell. It also meant that more cattle could be raised. Also, Ethiopia was trying to increase its exports to bring more foreign money into the country. There were even plans for additional and better roads.

But Ethiopia is a country of contradictions. Consider its name. For centuries, at least through the 1940s, many people living outside Ethiopia called it "Abyssinia," while most Ethiopians called it Ethiopia—except when they were talking to outsiders. Some experts think the name Abyssinia comes from one of the original tribal groups. The name Ethiopia comes from ancient Greek and means "sunburned."

Although Amharic is the official language of Ethiopia, more than seventy different languages are spoken. Often, a person who speaks one of the native languages meets a person who speaks a different native language; they may speak English or Italian to each other.

Religion is another one of Ethiopia's contradictions. Ethiopia has a national religion—Coptic Christianity—but many of the people are Moslems.

Ethiopia's government represents another contradiction. This country, with its long history of rulers believed to be descended from the Queen of Sheba and King Solomon, changed governments in 1974 in favor of a Communist government. The old government kept both power and wealth in the hands of a few families. In theory, a Communist government would spread the power and wealth throughout the country. The new rulers describe themselves as Marxist-Leninist, which is the strictest form of Communism as it has developed. Today, however, most of the people in Ethiopia are poorer than ever.

In addition, although Ethiopia is so much in the news, it is very difficult to know what is true. The government for a long time denied that any of the problems were really serious. They may have felt that admitting there were problems would make people think that the government wasn't any good. And Ethiopia has always been a secretive country.

Although many people believe that the present tragedy of Ethiopia was caused by the change in political systems, others do not agree. They feel that many of today's problems stem from actions by the upper classes and rulers in the past.

Many of these contradictions have created the problems that Ethiopia faces today. There are, for instance, civil wars. Most of these are in the parts of the country called Eritrea and Tigre. Wars mean troops for both sides who must be paid and fed and kept in clothes. Wars also mean less money and food and clothing for the rest of the population.

The Expanding Desert

The desert area of Ethiopia is growing larger. This is happening throughout much of North Africa as the Sahara expands into the fertile areas. In Ethiopia the problem is much more serious—or at least it is getting more publicity. This movement of the desert, combined with war, means that less food is being grown. And this means famine.

If a farmer plants crops that fail, and he can't buy food for his family either because he has no money or because there is no one to sell food to him, he and his family will starve. Since the entire area has been suffering from a drought, a long period with little or no rain, it is easy to see why food won't grow.

It might seem that none of this—except war—could be prevented. But many experts believe that both the spreading of the Sahara and the drought could have been made less serious by human action.

How? How could people prevent the desert moving? How could people make the rain fall?

Many experts agree that the drought didn't help but that the problems had other causes as well. Some of these are:

*Misuse of the land and severe droughts are causing
the desertification of northern Africa, as the
Sahara Desert spreads onto previously arable land.*

- Overgrazing. Grazing is the eating of naturally growing plant materials by animals, and overgrazing is letting them eat so much of the vegetation in an area that nothing new grows. Overgrazing causes rainwater to hit the ground and run quickly into rivers without soaking in. This means there is less evaporation of water from the land into rain clouds that could bring rain to water crops which would feed people.

- Overcultivation. This means farming an area of soil without replacing lost nutrients, either by letting the fields lie fallow regularly or with fertilizers.

- Overpopulation. As more people move into an area or are born, more food is required to feed them. This leads to overpopulation. In Ethiopia new populations have also cut down trees for houses or firewood without replanting them. This causes erosion and can have much the same effect as overgrazing.

Another cause of the tragedy is that the problem areas had much greater than usual rainfall during the 1950s. At that time, many people moved into parts of Ethiopia that had been mainly uncultivated in the past. When the drought started in 1968 the land could no longer provide enough food for all these people.

Some of the problems were caused by what seemed to be advances. For instance, many of these areas relied on rainfall for water and had no wells. It seemed a good idea to dig wells. When wells were dug, many cattle raisers were able to increase the size of their herds, which was fine until the drought came along and affected the natural vegetation. In the end, the animals died for lack of food, not water.

A herdsman with his flock in the drought-stricken village of Bume in 1974. About 85 percent of southern Ethiopia's cattle herds died during the 1974 drought.

These are some of the causes of the present situation. But this isn't the first time Ethiopia has suffered terrible drought—there were such droughts in the 1680s, 1750s, 1820s, 1910s, and probably earlier, for thousands of years.

Many experts warned that, with the way the land was being used, the next drought would lead to the situation that now exists. And experts from many parts of the world visited the edges of the Sahara and warned governments of what might happen. But most of the warnings were ignored.

Also, most governments are concerned with staying in power and they tend to do things that will keep them there. If the Ethiopian government had told the people to stop abusing the land, they might have lost power. Since the Communist government only came to power in 1974, they may have decided not to risk their power by telling the people to change their way of life.

Helping Ethiopia

Can something be done to help the starving people of Ethiopia? Yes, help can be sent and is being sent. Food is important, of course, but so is medicine to keep terrible diseases from sweeping the country. The greatest current danger is from cholera, a disease that spreads rapidly and causes stomach problems so serious that they weaken the person to the point of death.

The Ethiopian government says there are no cases of cholera. Many foreign experts helping in the country believe there are. Unfortunately, one of the most important ways of treating cholera (and similar diseases) is with fluids which are very scarce. Cholera is a dreadful disease, but if sufficient water and minerals are given to a patient that patient will recover. The drug tetracycline is effective against cholera, but only if given early in the disease.

Cholera is caused by unsanitary conditions. These are common when people are moving from place to place and do not make sure that their latrines are separated from their food and water. Cholera resembles other diseases with similar symptoms so health workers want to know when they are treating cholera. The refusal of Ethiopian officials to give the results of tests for cholera to health workers is making their job more difficult.

Cholera and many other diseases that are the result of poor sanitation are almost inevitable with a population that is on the move. Ethiopians have left the places they were living in to find food and water. These refugees are looking for new places to live, in Ethiopia or in nearby countries such as the Sudan.

Among the groups that are doing excellent work in Ethiopia are the Red Cross, World Vision, Catholic Relief, World Food, and the United Nations Relief Organization. All these groups need money to carry on their work. The sad side of this picture is that other groups have been raising money for Ethiopia but spending a lot of it on other things—such as on paying the people who run the organizations.

Sacks of grain donated by the European Economic Community being unloaded at a relief center. Organizations and nations around the world quickly came to the aid of Ethiopia and other African countries, but the current famine remains the continent's most urgent problem.

A very bright side to the relief question has been the way musicians have responded to the need. First in Great Britain, then in the United States, rock stars have put out special records and given concerts, donating the proceeds to aid for Ethiopia and other drought-stricken countries in Africa.

Is it enough? No. One estimate is that a billion dollars would be needed to feed Africans in one year. But it is a wonderful example of people working together to help Africa.

Money raised by the Live-Aid rock concert was given to African famine relief. The concert, staged simultaneously in London and Philadelphia on July 15, 1985, was beamed via satellite to 160 countries worldwide.

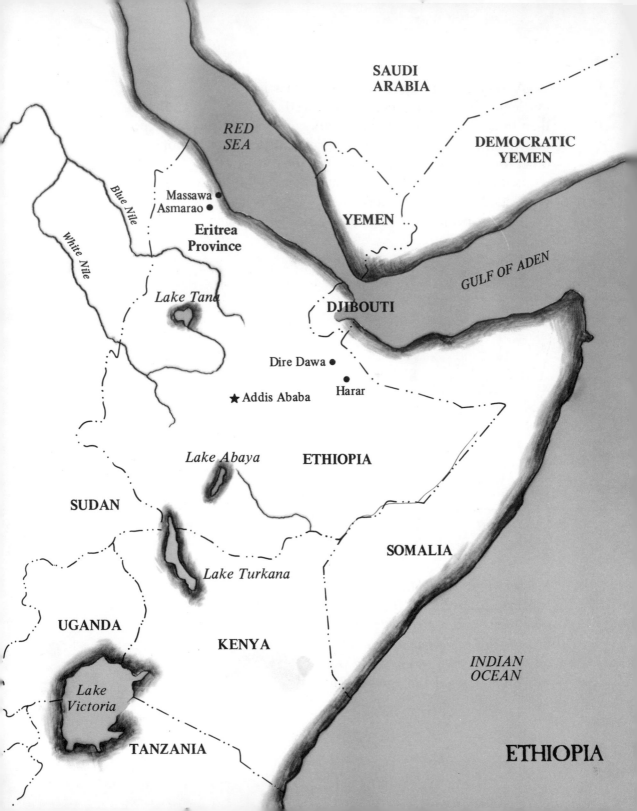

SAUDI
ARABIA

*RED
SEA*

DEMOCRATIC
YEMEN

Blue Nile

White Nile

Massawa ●
Asmara ○

**Eritrea
Province**

YEMEN

GULF OF ADEN

Lake Tana

DJIBOUTI

Dire Dawa ●
● Harar

★ Addis Ababa

Lake Abaya

ETHIOPIA

SUDAN

Lake Turkana

SOMALIA

UGANDA

KENYA

*INDIAN
OCEAN*

*Lake
Victoria*

TANZANIA

ETHIOPIA

CHAPTER 2

GEOGRAPHY'S EFFECT

Geography is very important in shaping the history of a country and Ethiopia is no exception. Ethiopia, which is about four-fifths the size of Alaska, is in Africa. Africa is usually thought of as being very hot, but Ethiopia is a country with mountains as high as 15,000 feet (4,572 m) and high, large plateaus. Ethiopia borders the Red Sea, the Sudan, Uganda, Kenya, the Somali Republic, and Djibouti, formerly the French Territory of Afars and the Issas.

Ethiopia is located on the Horn of Africa. A map of Africa shows in the northeast a section that gradually narrows to form almost a point. That is called the Horn, and Ethiopia is located on the point where it begins to form. (Early explorers and map makers found that naming things by the way they looked made them easier to remember.)

Ethiopia has had a long history of independence. Unlike most nations of Africa, including Egypt, Morocco, Kenya, and Cameroon, Ethiopia never belonged to a colonial power such as Great Britain or France. Except for occupation and rule by Italy for five years from 1936 to 1941, Ethiopia has been independent for almost three thousand years.

Geography played a part in this independence. It was hard to get troops across a land surrounded by desert and hard to get soldiers up the plateaus. Thus, conquering the land was difficult. Italy succeeded in the twentieth century because it used modern military equipment including airplanes.

The geography of Ethiopia is somewhat similar to that of Mexico. They both have plateau areas, and the Ethiopian plateaus have excellent rainfall. Mexico City and Addis Ababa, Ethiopia's capital, are both about 8,000 feet (2,438 m) above sea level.

For both Mexico and Ethiopia, their high plateaus give them a temperature that is neither very hot nor very cold—most of the time. Temperate climates are good for growing things and pleasant for people. And because they are near the equator, neither Addis Ababa nor Mexico City has seasons the way most of the United States does, which means crops can be grown all year round. These high plateau areas have another advantage—they are fairly free of the mosquitoes that carry malaria, a common disease of the tropics. The plateau areas of Ethiopia have traditionally been fertile, comfortable to live in, and prosperous.

The Great Rift

One way in which Ethiopia differs from other countries with high, flat-topped mountains is that Ethiopia has what is known as

The Ethiopian plateau region in the northwestern part of the country

the Great Rift Valley. The valley runs from southwest Asia to east central Africa and crosses through Ethiopia from northeast to southwest. The Great Rift Valley is one of the reasons that movement and communication among the people are difficult. In addition to the two major plateaus on either side of the Great Rift Valley, there are many similar ones surrounded by deep ravines. These ravines have isolated the people on the plateaus.

Other Areas

In addition to these high plateaus, however, Ethiopia has flat desert land where little can be grown. Next to the desert are some areas that until recently were comparatively fertile. It is these areas where the land has become less and less fertile due to lack of rain and overuse. Eventually this land becomes desert where little or nothing will grow.

Since the desert areas are so barren the people there are poor. Some have left the areas for more fertile lands, including the cities, but most of the people have stayed in the land where they were born even though it can no longer support them. In Ethiopia there is a big division between the rich or at least fairly well off people in the cities and the poor in the desert areas.

The Nile

Explorers in previous centuries searched for the source, or starting point, of major rivers. One of the rivers for which they wanted to find the source was the Nile, the river that runs through Egypt and makes parts of it fertile.

The Nile was found to originate in Lake Tana, in northwest Ethiopia, where what is now called the Blue Nile begins. The other major river contributing to the Nile is now called the White

Tessissat Falls on Lake Tana,
the source of the Nile

Nile. It starts in Lake Victoria, on the common border of Uganda, Tanzania, and Kenya.

In normal times, when very heavy rains go into the Blue Nile, over half the flood waters in the Nile are contributed by the Blue Nile. The drought in Ethiopia has naturally affected the Nile.

Outlet to the Sea

There was, however, one thing that Ethiopia lacked until 1952. That was an outlet to the sea.

In 1952 the United Nations decided that Eritrea, which like Ethiopia was briefly occupied by Italy and had been part of Ethiopia at various times in the past, should be federated with Ethiopia. This gave the Ethiopians two seaports on the Red Sea. Some of the Eritreans have been fighting for their independence ever since, and this is at least one reason for the civil wars.

Natural Resources

For many countries, certain natural resources such as gold and silver were of major importance. Even though Ethiopia is an ancient country, little or no wealth has been found by digging into the ground. There have been stories about gold and other minerals found in Ethiopia all the way back to the time of the Queen of Sheba (about 1000 B.C.), but these stories are mostly legendary. There are some known deposits of valuable minerals—but they haven't been mined because Ethiopia lacks the technology to make mining them profitable.

What is mined? Salt (which is valuable), but other items such as potash, talc, and copper lie more or less neglected in the ground.

The Ethiopian economy is based on farming. In normal times 90 percent of the people are either farming or raising animals to support themselves.

Most of the cattle belong to the zebu family, an East Indian humped ox. Traditionally they have been raised for prestige in many places rather than for food. They do provide milk and butter. Sheep and goats are raised for food. But many of these animals have starved recently.

Coffee grows wild in Ethiopia but it is also cultivated. In fact the name coffee comes from Kaffa, a province of Ethiopia. Coffee is Ethiopia's largest export and is very important, even today, to the American coffee industry. Other exports include spices, animal hides and skins, and seeds that are pressed for oil.

CHAPTER 3

ETHIOPIA'S
STORY

An incredible amount has been written about Ethiopia in the past, some of which was true and some of which was only legend.

Herodotus, a Greek who lived around 450 B.C. and who many believe started the idea of written history, wrote in his *Histories* that "the Ethiopians are said to be the tallest and handsomest people in the world." He also thought they—or at least their rulers—were smart. He told the story of an Ethiopian king who, visited by men pretending to be friends, realized they were spies for the king of Persia.

The men brought presents. There was a scarlet robe—the king said that since it was dyed the robe was false. There were gold chains and bracelets—the king insisted they weren't ornaments but were used to hold prisoners and said that Ethiopia had stronger ones. And there was myrrh. He said that was false, too, as it was used as a perfume to hide natural odors.

Herodotus wasn't writing history the way it is written today, with very specific information about dates. And Herodotus didn't always separate legend from truth—but he did tell a good story.

Queen of Sheba

Many people believe Ethiopia was founded by the Queen of Sheba and King Solomon of Israel. The story of the Queen of Sheba's visit to King Solomon is told in the Bible. She was obviously a very wealthy queen and most experts agree that she did come from Ethiopia—that Sheba later became Ethiopia.

The Bible says she made her visit to test Solomon's wisdom by asking him difficult questions. She brought him gifts of spices, gold, and precious stones. King Solomon impressed her with his answers to her questions and they exchanged more gifts.

As is the case with many countries that were founded a long time ago, there is disagreement about exactly when Ethiopia was founded. Ethiopians date the founding of their country from the reign of the Queen of Sheba's son, around 1000 B.C. At this time, Ethiopia was probably called Aksum.

But some people believe Ethiopia wasn't founded until around A.D. 100. One theory is that it was founded by southern Arabian immigrants, mostly traders, who began settling there around 500 B.C. In the fourth century A.D., Aksum, led by King Ezana, was converted to Christianity. At that time, the country ruled the Red Sea coast and probably traded with countries in the Mediterranean.

Religion in Ethiopia's Past

The Christianity of Ethiopia is what is called Coptic Christianity. This is a branch of Christianity that grew out of an argument in the fifth century A.D. over whether Jesus was of one nature— divine only—which the founders of Coptic Christianity believed, or two natures—human and divine—which the rest of Christianity believed.

This controversy led to Coptic Christianity moving away from the mainstream of the religion. Over the centuries, from time to time, there have been meetings of the two sides in attempts to join together again, but so far they have not been successful.

Coptic Christianity was also the religion in other countries, such as Egypt. Missionaries went from Aksum to other countries to convert people to their form of Christianity, with some success. The sixth century was a time of great religious interest in general and there was also interest in Judaism in Aksum. Some experts believe Jewish traders who settled there converted native Ethiopians to Judaism.

Other experts believe that the Ethiopian Jews are descendants of the ancient Israel tribe of Dan, which left Israel in a time of trouble and settled in Ethiopia. And some believe that the Ethiopian Jews are the only true descendants of King Solomon and the Queen of Sheba.

The Ethiopian Jews are called Falashas by other Ethiopians and by people who don't realize the Jews consider the word an insult. It means strangers but not in a friendly way—more in the sense of outsiders. The Ethiopian Jews call themselves Beth Israel, which means House of Israel, and want other people to call them that, too.

Islam, also called Mohammedism or Moslemism, is the religion founded by Mohammed, who lived from about A.D. 570 to about A.D. 632. In the seventh century, Islam began to move across

According to the popular legend,
Ethiopia was founded by the Queen
of Sheba and King Solomon.

North Africa. Aksum lost power, partly because its control of the trade routes of the Red Sea ended as Islam, which is a religion that rules both the spiritual and political lives of believers, moved in.

This changed Aksum greatly. Where Aksum had previously been a country that looked outward—to the sea—it now looked inward to the Ethiopian plateau and was cut off from developments outside. Soon the country was no longer united but became divided into small units which often had their own leaders.

The family of the original rulers (sometimes called the Solomonic family) was overthrown in 1137 but came back to power in 1270.

The Renaissance

The restoration of the Solomonic family to the throne brought out the talent of the country. From 1270 until the middle 1500s many forms of art flourished.

Since it was a religious period, this outpouring of talent—often called the Ethiopian Renaissance—was seen mainly in religious pictures, book illustrations, writing, and sculpture. The government and the religion were closely knit, and the country had strength and unity again.

The Ethiopian Renaissance ended in the mid-1500s when the country was exhausted by a war with the Somalis. With the help of Portugal, Ethiopia eventually won the war but the war had cost so much in money, lives, and energy that the Renaissance was over.

Before this time there had been many attempts to win the country away from Christianity and to Islam. In some parts of what is now Ethiopia—especially the south and northeast—

people did convert to Islam, but Coptic Christianity remained the main religion.

In most countries in North Africa, however, Islam became the state religion. When even Egypt, which had been a major Christian country, became Islamic in the seventh century, Ethiopia began to feel—as it did for centuries afterward—that it was a Christian oasis in an Islamic desert.

Portugal was an important explorer nation in the sixteenth century and a Portuguese embassy (a group of people sent by a friendly foreign nation) arrived at the Ethiopian court in 1520. Later, when a Muslim general from Somali conquered large parts of Ethiopia, the emperor—sometimes called the Negus, the native word for emperor—asked Portugal for help, which was sent.

The Somali troops were defeated, but the war ended the Rennaissance and left the country weak enough for other people to make successful small invasions.

Other Emperors

In 1622 the emperor Susenyos was converted not to Islam as might be expected but to Roman Catholicism—the group which believed Jesus was both human and divine. But the Coptic clergy and the Ethiopian nobility refused to be converted. In the end they forced this emperor to abdicate, or to give up his throne.

His son Fasilidas became emperor, threw out the Roman Catholic clergymen, reestablished the Coptic Church, and closed Ethiopia to all foreigners. Meanwhile, there were civil wars (similar to those going on now) among various princes.

One successful prince conquered the areas of Amhara, Gojjam, Tigre, and Shoa and was crowned Emperor Theo-

*Ruins of the castle built for
Emperor Fasilidas in the seventeenth century.
On the right is the city of Gondor.*

dore II in 1855. As emperor he modernized and centralized several government systems.

At the end of his life he became insane or, at least, bad tempered. He wrote a letter to Queen Victoria of Great Britain and when she didn't answer it quickly enough he threw several British subjects, including the British consul, in jail. The British were outraged. They sent troops, the Ethiopians were defeated, and Theodore killed himself so he wouldn't be captured.

Much of the history of Ethiopia for the rest of the nineteenth century is one of civil wars and attempts by foreign countries to colonize the land. Powers that included Italy, France, and Great Britain tried to influence Ethiopia because of the opening of the Suez Canal in the middle of the century. This canal joined the Mediterranean and the Red Seas and made the country easier to reach.

Italy invaded in 1895 but, under Emperor Menelik II, Ethiopian troops defeated the Italians. Menelik II did a great deal to bring Ethiopia up to date. He added land (the provinces of Hara, Sidamo, and Kaffa), modernized the army and the government, improved the economy, encouraged the building of a railroad, began the postal service, and moved the capital to Addis Ababa.

Menelik died in 1916; his grandson succeeded him but was overthrown. He was succeeded by Judith, a daughter of Menelik, who was followed in 1930 by Haile Selassie I.

Haile Selassie

Haile Selassie is undoubtedly the best-known modern ruler of Ethiopia. Italy had long been one of the countries that wanted control of Ethiopia, and in 1935 it decided to make its move. Italy invaded the country on October 3, 1935.

Ethiopia had joined the League of Nations in 1923. The League was similar in ideals to the United Nations and Haile Selassie went to the League and begged it for help against Italy. The result was not really much help. The League called for economic sanctions—measures restricting trade with Italy—that didn't bother Italy one bit. Some people think this led to the final failure of the League of Nations.

Armed with modern weapons and airplanes, Italy captured Ethiopia in May 1936, and Haile Selassie fled to Great Britain. Since Italy already had Eritrea, it merged Eritrea with Ethiopia and Italian Somaliland, forming the colony of Italian East Africa.

The occupation didn't last long. In World War II (1939–1945), British and South African troops defeated the Italians in Ethiopia in 1941, and Haile Selassie returned home. Ethiopia joined the United Nations as a charter member in 1945. Eritrea became part of Ethiopia in 1952.

Never at Peace?

But that wasn't the end of the story. Ethiopia seems to be a country that can never be at peace for long.

In 1960, while Haile Selassie was visiting Brazil, his government was overthrown, but he was restored to power a few days after he returned to Ethiopia.

In 1938 emperor-in-exile Haile Selassie petitioned the League of Nations in Geneva to denounce the Italian occupation of his country. His efforts were fruitless, however, as the League voted 11–3 in favor of recognizing Italy's claim.

One theory of keeping power is to have weak people around to help rule. The idea is that strong people might get the idea that they could rule better and decide to overthrow the government. Weak people, on the other hand, would stay in their places. Many people believe Haile Selassie deliberately had weak ministers around him for this reason and that because they were weak, many needed reforms never took place. The strong people got mad about this and decided to do something about it.

Then too, almost from the beginning of their union with Ethiopia, people in Eritrea wanted to be independent. They have sometimes fought in what we consider the usual way but more often have used guerilla tactics, with small, independent bands staging quick and unexpected attacks.

Haile Selassie regained his throne after the short-lived coup d'état (a violent change of government) in 1960, but he only stayed in power until 1974 when he was overthrown again—this time by a group of military officers. Some of the reasons given for this coup were the excess power of the ruling class and the need for such changes as more education. When this group formed its government, they promised to reform society.

Many people also believe Haile Selassie was overthrown because of a drought in northern Ethiopia from 1973 to 1974 during which many people starved to death. Some say Haile Selassie's failure to take action to prevent the starvation influenced people against him.

Emperor Haile Selassie met
with Richard Nixon at the
White House in 1970

At present, the ruler of Ethiopia is Mengistu Haile Mariam. The government has declared itself to be Marxist-Leninist Communist and therefore tends to look to such Communist countries as the Soviet Union as its friends.

CHAPTER 4

HISTORY
REPEATS

There's a saying, very true, that history repeats itself. This is certainly true in the case of the recent history of Ethiopia. The very things for which Haile Selassie was overthrown are happening now under the new government.

It's very difficult to find out about Ethiopia. Haile Selassie and most of the emperors before him discouraged people from writing about the country. Today's present rulers are doing the same thing.

Then and Now

In 1974, when Haile Selassie was overthrown, the situation for the people was almost the same as it is today.

There was a drought and people were starving.

And the reason they were starving wasn't because there was no food in the country but because speculators (people who buy something at a low price and hang on to it expecting it will go to a higher price) had bought up the food and were storing it or offering to sell it for much more than people could afford. Since Ethiopia was and is such a closed country, few people were aware of the starvation in the north.

During the early 1970s Jonathan Dimbleby, a British television journalist, had made films about Ethiopia that the government liked. When he asked permission to make another film, Haile Selassie granted it.

The result was a film shown on television in Britain and then in many other parts of the world called *Ethiopia: The Unknown Famine*. The film showed starving people lying in the road—and planes carrying expensive wine and food to Haile Selassie. It showed skeletonlike people—and the emperor feeding meat to his dogs from silver platters.

More Journalists

This happened in 1973 and it woke up the world. Newspapers began publishing as much accurate information as they could get—but they couldn't get much.

Journalists flew into Ethiopia from all over to see what was happening but the government wouldn't let them go to the north, where the starvation was (and where it is today) because, they said, there were bandits there. The journalists didn't know whether or not there were really bandits, but they wanted to see for themselves.

Instead, the journalists were taken around to see Ethiopia's showpieces, such as new buildings. In the end, photographs of the starving people were smuggled to journalists and, since they never did get north, the journalists had to be content. Of course, they weren't content at all and, in addition to publishing the photographs, they published all the rumors about the true situation and the truth about the attempts to hide it.

Relief missions began arriving in Ethiopia—just as is happening now. And some of the relief organizations said that some shipments of food for the starving people weren't reaching them —just as is being said today. The last straw for the relief organizations was when they were ordered to pay high customs duties on these food shipments.

Gradually there was more and more trouble. Soldiers rebelled against their officers, students rioted, and eventually an army group called the Armed Forces Coordinating Committee deposed Haile Selassie.

On the day he was deposed, Selassie was quoted as saying, "If the revolution is good for the people, then I am for the revolution." Some people wonder if he really said that or, if he said it, if he really meant it.

He was moved from the official palace to another palace (not prison) where he died on August 27, 1975, of "circulatory failure." He was eighty-four years old.

Ethiopian Governments

What type of government did the Ethiopians have before Haile Selassie was overthrown? They considered themselves a monarchy with a hereditary emperor who was advised by his Council of Ministers.

There was a bicameral legislature—like the Senate and House of Representatives—but only the lower one was elected, and some experts say very few people voted or were allowed to vote.

That was the "official" view of the government. Most experts say that Ethiopia was an absolute monarchy: what the emperor wanted was all that mattered.

Mengistu Haile Mariam (left) shakes hands with his Sudanese counterpart, General Swareddahab, upon arriving at a meeting of the Organization of African Unity held in Addis Ababa in July 1985. Mariam, a leader of the 1974 army uprising that overthrew Selassie, is the current ruler of Ethiopia.

The emperor also appointed the prime minister, the governors, the mayors, the judges, and the senators and had a certain amount of control over the state Coptic Christian church. Although some reforms were made in the government with a new constitution in 1955 (such as the possible impeachment of officials charged with wrongdoing and direct voting for the lower part of the legislature), the emperor was still the most important governing force.

Today's government is difficult to learn about. It considers itself Marxist-Leninist, and Communist countries of this type are never eager to let the rest of the world know what they are doing. Ethiopia, in any case, has always been secretive unless it was to its advantage to allow foreigners in to see it.

As often happens when governments change, the life of the ordinary person, or even of the very wealthy Ethiopian, has probably not changed very much. The emperor is gone and so are the people who worked closely with him, but in his place is a leader, Mengistu Haile Mariam, with very much the same power and the same governmental system as the emperor.

Corruption, for example, selling donated grain, is probably the same as it was under the emperor, and there's no question that there is as great an indifference to the starving people as there was in 1973.

And again, Ethiopia is trying to hide the extent of its problems.

CHAPTER 5

THE ETHIOPIAN PEOPLE

The Ethiopian people are made up of many different groups who originally lived in many different places. These groups have stayed remarkably separate from each other (as compared to the immigrants who came to the United States, for instance). They have their own language, live mainly in their own areas, and have their own ways of life. Few people marry outside the groups.

The Beja people are thought to have been in Ethiopia the longest. They are believed to have come to Ethiopa thousands of years ago. Many of the Beja people are settled in northwest Ethiopia. The Sidama who live south of the high plateau are related to the Bejas.

Nomads

Ethiopia has many nomadic groups. Nomads are groups of people who don't live in any one place. Instead, they travel from place to place looking for food and water for themselves and their animals. If they find a place they like they may stay there for a while until the food starts to run out or they grow restless. There are many nomads in desert parts of the world.

Every so often, some country or some people will persuade nomads to settle in one place. They may stay for a time, but after a while they miss their traveling life and start on it again. This is fine—so long as there is plenty of grazing and plenty of water to be found.

In Ethiopia there are several nomadic groups who live on the plains east of the plateau. These groups—all of whom are considered Beja—are the Danakils, the Gallas, and the Somalis.

Semites

Another group of people who came to Ethiopia long ago were the Semites. They came from the southern part of Arabia. They mingled with the people already there and in many cases their language, called Ge'ez or Ethiopic, became predominant. They settled originally in the east but moved their grazing to central and southern Ethiopia in the 1500s.

The Amharics are another group of people and the ones who have been most important in ruling the country over the years. They are highlanders from the Ethiopian plateau and are believed to be a mixture of Semitic and Hamitic (a similar group) backgrounds. Together with the Tigreans, who are also of Semitic background, they make up about one-third of the people.

The Galla people are of Hamitic background. Traditionally they have lived in the desert area. About 40 percent of the Ethiopian people belong to this group.

The Shankali people, who account for 6 percent of Ethiopia's population, are on the western frontier. There are also the Somalis in the east and southeast representing another 6 percent.

Beth Israel, the Jewish group, was in the mountains south of Tigre. Many of them fled the famine to the Sudan where the Israeli government arranged for some of them to be flown to Israel. The United States followed up with additional flights.

There are other Hamitic groups, some of whom live in the same place and speak the same language—usually a language that cannot be understood by other groups.

At one time a large number of foreigners lived in Ethiopia, mainly in Addis Ababa. They included Arabs, Italians, Armenians, Greeks, and Indians from India.

There was also another group of people in Ethiopia—slaves of various backgrounds. Slavery and slave labor were an important part of Ethiopian life until very recently. In order to join the League of Nations (which it did in 1923), Ethiopia had to agree to the St. Germain convention in favor of the end of slavery and the slave trade. Although Ethiopia signed the treaty, most experts believe that there was slavery in Ethiopia for many years after that.

Some people believe the Italians actually abolished slavery during their occupation. However, Haile Selassie issued a formal proclamation abolishing slavery in 1942.

Rapid Changes

Because of the combination of drought, hunger, war, and perhaps disease, the population is not only moving around the country trying to get away from the problems but is also fleeing

Nomads in the
Ethiopian plains

into nearby countries such as the Sudan. Understandably, the number of foreigners has fallen greatly in recent years.

The people who have been affected most by the troubles are, of course, those from desert areas.

Farming

How do or did these people live? Many of them live what we would consider a very primitive life.

The modern farming we see in the United States has always been rare if not nonexistent in Ethiopia. There the people practice inefficient subsistence farming which provides barely enough food for a single family.

The main crops are millet (a grasslike plant with very nutritious seeds), sorghum (a plant similar to millet), barley, wheat, corn, plantain (a plant somewhat similar to a banana), peas, potatoes, coffee, peanuts, cotton, sugar cane, and tobacco. Animals that are raised include poultry, cattle, sheep, and goats.

Crops such as coffee and cotton aren't used by the grower— they are sold or traded for other things the farmer needs. Most subsistence farmers grow only what they can use.

Farming is always hard work, but it's especially hard when you have to do everything, including plowing, planting, weeding, and harvesting, by hand. Often water must be brought long distances. Everyone in the subsistence farmer's family who is old enough (which can be as young as three years old) works the farm.

City Life

Some Ethiopians live in cities, such as the capital, Addis Ababa. The poor live in mud and thatched huts like the ones many people live in in the rest of the country. The richer people have modern houses and some of them enjoy movies, television, radio, and telephones. In these cities there are shops and stands where things can be bought.

Bargaining is an important part of shopping in the cities. If you ask how much something costs, a vendor will always answer with a very high price—higher than he or she expects to get. You will then offer a very low price—much lower than you expect to pay. Gradually, the prices get closer and closer together until you and the seller come to a price that you both think is fair.

Business and Industry

Some people in Ethiopia work in the government. Others work in manufacturing. They work in textiles, sugar and food processing, meat packing, leather and shoes, and in manufacturing vegetable oil, cookies, and macaroni. Other workers not in factories are silversmiths, carpenters, and basket makers.

Ethiopia, like many hot countries, has siestas so people can eat lunch and take a nap during the hottest part of the day. Business hours in the cities are generally from 9:00 A.M. to 1:00 P.M. and from 3:00 P.M. to 6:00 P.M.

Ethiopia does have electricity, although not everywhere. Since there are no deposits of coal or similar materials to produce the electricity, water power is used instead.

Most Ethiopians never go to school. Ninety percent of the people, many reports say, can't read or write. Most parts of the country have no schools at all and, in any case, people of school age would probably have to work to help their families.

There are schools in the cities. Where there are state-funded public schools the education is free from elementary school through college.

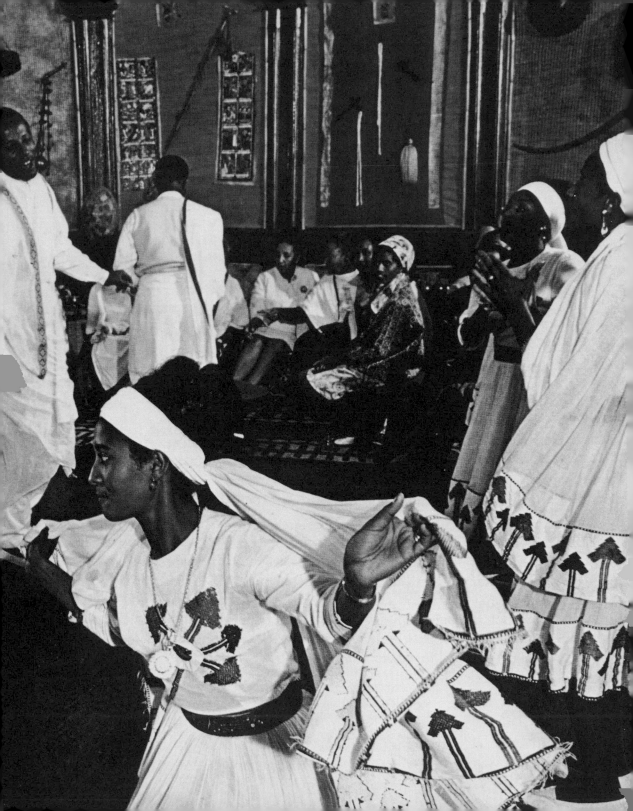

Houses and Clothes

Many people, even in cities, live in mud huts and often there is only one room for a family. The mud is claylike and is baked, usually by the sun, into bricks to build the hut. Or it is used like cement to form the entire building. This type of mud is used all over North Africa and some buildings made from it have lasted thousands of years.

Most people wear draped clothing. One single piece of fabric is arranged around the body instead of being cut into pieces and then sewn together as our clothes are. Draped clothes are very practical. They are easy to layer for warmth (in parts of Ethiopia the temperature drops thirty degrees Fahrenheit between noon and midnight). And draped clothes can be used as covers at night.

Transportation

Transportation has always been poor in Ethiopia. There are only three railroad lines and these may have been destroyed or damaged in the recent wars. One railroad goes from Addis Ababa to Djibouti (formerly the French Territory of Afars and the Issas). Another is in Eritrea and connects Massawa with Asmara and Agordate. There is a third railroad that connects the Awash Valley with Port Assab.

There are about 5,000 miles (8,047 km) of good "all weather" roads; one-third of these have an asphalt surface. The

Folk dancers in a
restaurant in Addis Ababa

others are made of gravel and earth, gravel, or crushed stone. About 10,000 miles (16,093 km) of road are made entirely of earth. These can be used only in dry weather. Most roads go from Addis Ababa and Asmara to the main producing areas and to the port cities of Assab and Massawa.

Many parts of the world jumped from the age of the camel or horse to the age of the airplane, almost skipping railroads and automobiles. To a certain extent, this was the case with Ethiopia. The plateaus were connected by the airplane; mail, food, and heavy cargo, which could not easily get to these places otherwise, arrived by plane. The advances that were being made by flights of this kind within Ethiopia have been slowed by the current problems.

CHAPTER 6

RELIGION AND LANGUAGE IN ETHIOPIA

Ethiopia is now a Marxist-Leninist Communist country, and most Communist countries discourage religion. Although some reports of religious persecution have come out of Ethiopia, few experts believe that it was actually led by the government.

We can probably assume that religion, while certainly not encouraged in Ethiopia, is not being stamped out by the government.

The official religion of Ethiopia for centuries was Coptic Christianity. This church became very wealthy over the years and this wealth may have angered some people and contributed to the coups d'état against the government.

Although Coptic Christianity was the official religion, there are probably more Moslems than Christians in the country. Most people in North Africa are Moslem.

Islam

Islam completely rules the lives of its believers, affecting everything from politics to art to a much greater extent than does a

Villagers congregate at an Ethiopian Orthodox church.
Although Ethiopia officially broke away
from Coptic Christianity in 1959,
the new religion, called Ethiopian Orthodox,
has strong ties to Coptic Christianity.

religion such as Christianity. The Koran, which is a collection of God's revelations to Mohammed, is Islam's supreme source for how to live. There are other writings which are also used. How strictly Islam is practiced varies from country to country and from person to person.

Other Beliefs

We've already mentioned the Jews of Ethiopia, called Falashas (a rude word) by other Ethiopians and Beth Israel by themselves. Over many years they managed to keep to their religion and customs, including teaching their children to read Hebrew.

A large number of Ethiopians have animistic beliefs, ones which give spiritual characteristics to just about everything. This means that animists believe that stones, mountains, plants, and, in some cases, such things as dreams have spirits in them.

Amharic

The official language of Ethiopia is Amharic. Amharic is the language of the Amharic people who ruled the country for many years and who lived on the plateau where Addis Ababa is located.

What is Amharic like?

It is very different from the languages most of us know which come from Latin and European roots. Amharic is one of the Hamito-Semitic languages (a group of languages that includes Hebrew and Arabic) which most scholars believe started as one language and gradually turned into many. Several other Hamito-Semitic languages, in addition to Amharic, are spoken in Ethiopia.

The same thing happened to Latin, of course, which evolved into such languages as French, Spanish, Portuguese, and Italian.

በዓለም ፡ ላይ ፡ በሚነገር ፡ በማናቸውም ፡
ቋንቋ ፡ የተጻፈ ፡ መጽሐፍ ፡ ማተም ፡ የሚችል ፡
እስቲፍን ፡ አስቲንና ፡ ልጆቹ ፡ ሊሚትድ ፡
ብቻ ፡ ነው ።

An example of written Amharic

Ethiopic

Amharic comes from a language called Ethiopic. This language is still used by the Coptic Christian Church for its religious services—just as the Jewish religion uses ancient Hebrew and, until recently, the Roman Catholic Church used Latin. Ethiopic is called Ge'ez or Classic Ethiopic and most of the great writings of the Ethiopian Renaissance were in this language.

Ethiopic and Amharic are syllabic languages. This means that in writing, one sign represents one syllable. English uses one or more letters to make individual sounds. These letters are put together to form syllables. Syllabic languages are considered much more difficult to learn to read and write than alphabetic languages, such as English.

Although Amharic, the official language, and Ethiopic, the language of Coptic Christianity, both have written forms, most of the other Ethiopian languages do not.

Lingua Franca

What do people do in countries where many different languages are spoken?

All over Africa there are small tribal groups living, usually, isolated from each other. When they meet, they can't talk to each other unless they have a common language—not their original language but a language that everyone knows something about.

In other parts of Africa, Hausa, Swahili, and Pidgin English (a simplified form of English) are used. This type of language is called a *lingua franca*. These languages usually aren't the mother tongue of any of the people using them, but they work. Although you might expect Amharic to be the *lingua franca* of everyone in Ethiopia, not enough people go to school to learn it.

Instead, English (partly because British and South African troops were in the country during the Second World War) and Italian (because the Italians ruled the country from 1936 to 1941) are used. This doesn't mean that everyone in the country knows these languages, of course, but the people who have reason to meet with people from other language groups will know at least some of one or the other.

CHAPTER 7

ETHIOPIA'S FUTURE

The story of Ethiopia today seems a sad one without hope. Even if the drought ended tomorrow it would be a year or two before the country would recover, and even then many things might not change.

It seems likely that there would still be terribly poor people and terribly rich people. The rich people would probably continue to rule the country. The country would still be divided by steep ravines leading down from and up to the plateaus and by different languages and religions. And the Sahara would continue to overtake once-fertile land.

But this doesn't have to be. And it's possible that the present government—which came to power as a reform government—may be able to improve things. And if the present government doesn't, another government may come in that does.

Planning for the Future

Many people know what needs to be done. Their dreams for Ethiopia include:

- more landing fields so more airplanes could carry passengers and items from one area to another area
- more all-year roads for the same reason
- more use of irrigation of crops, so that dry areas could use water from wet areas
- strict control so that food would not be used to make some people rich while others are starving
- more friendship among the different groups of people to help understanding
- more knowledge of Amharic or English or Italian so people from different areas can understand each other
- more help for farmers—perhaps through common ownership of such tools as tractors—so they can grow more food than just what they personally need
- better-educated farmers who can understand the role of soil nutrients, the best crops to grow for each area, and ways to improve their animals
- health education including sanitation, germ theory, and care of pregnant women and babies
- preventive medicine to fight the common diseases
- isolation areas for the sick to prevent the spread of disease
- education in forestry conservation to teach replanting as trees are felled and efficient ways to do it
- schools everywhere, for children at least up to age twelve. (Many people would put this item at the top of a list like this but until Ethiopian children have enough to eat and drink schools will have to wait.)
- better housing

Changing

None of these changes will happen overnight unless the government decides to act. Such change usually works best when it

happens gradually and people accept improved ways willingly, rather than by force.

Even with all the improvements needed, most Ethiopians would probably continue to live much the same lives as they do now. Their lives should be as pleasant as possible, without either the threat of starvation or too rapid change.

There are some things that make Ethiopia's future look brighter than one might expect, knowing its history. There has been a tremendous amount of true loving concern and practical help from individual people, from charities, from religious groups, and from governments outside Ethiopia.

Although Ethiopia's government has been trying to hide its problems from the world, it can't hide them from itself. The government must realize that, even after the famine ends, the country will still be one of rich and poor with, from a practical standpoint, a chance for revolution from the poor once they are strong enough to revolt.

Although once the crisis is over most of the relief organizations will probably leave Ethiopia to go somewhere else that's in trouble, some of them will undoubtedly stay. These groups will be known and trusted by the people. They will be able to help effect some of the necessary changes.

For many Ethiopians, planning for the future means trying to make sure there will be something to eat tomorrow. If they—and the nation as a whole— are to have a brighter future, the current government must begin an intense program of economic and social improvements.

Ethiopia may never again be the closed country it once was. The world knows about Ethiopia—perhaps not as much as it would like to, but still a lot—and when this famine is over the world will be watching to see what Ethiopia does to prevent future famines. This may cut down on corruption and it may force Ethiopia to finally think of all its people.

GLOSSARY

Most unfamiliar words are defined where they are used in this book. This glossary contains those words that are most important to understanding Ethiopia.

Abyssinia—former name for Ethiopia

Amharic—the official language of Ethiopia

Beth Israel—House of Israel; name preferred by Ethiopian Jews

Coptic Christianity—a form of Christianity believing that Jesus was only divine, not human and divine

coup d'état—a sudden attempt to overthrow a government, usually by people within the government

erosion—wearing away, especially of fertile soil by rain

falashas—name for Ethiopian Jews; see Beth Israel

Ge'ez—early version of Amharic language, also called Ethiopic

Islam—religion based on the teachings of Mohammed

lingua franca—a common language used by people speaking different languages. In Ethiopia, English and Italian are both used as *lingua franca.*

Moslem—see Islam

Negus—the word for emperor in Amharic

nomads—people who live by moving themselves and their animals from fertile place to fertile place

oasis—fertile spot in a desert

plateau—a flat-topped mountain

renaissance—a period in which talent of all kinds, especially artistic, flowers

source—the place where a river begins

zebu—a hump-backed ox

FOR MORE INFORMATION

For most countries we could tell you that there are lots of good books you can read and tell you which ones we think are best. This isn't the case with Ethiopia.

In the first place, things are changing very rapidly in Ethiopia. In the second place, there has never been much true information coming out of that country.

But don't give up. Newspapers and newsmagazines publish articles about Ethiopia fairly regularly. If you cut them out and keep them, you can compare them later to decide which stories report what seems to be going on and which stories might be just guesses.

INDEX

Illiteracy. *See* Literacy rate
Immigration, 42
Imports, 62–63, 66–68
Industry, 43
Islam. *See* Moslems; Koran
Israel, 41
Italian East Africa, 28
Italian Somaliland, 28
Italy, 13, 27, 28, 41, 51

Jews, Ethiopian, 23, 41, 49
Jobs, 43
Journalists, 34. *See also*
    Secrecy and government
Judith, Empress, 27

Koran, 49

Languages, 49–51, 53
League of Nations, 31, 41
Legend, 20
Lingua franca, 51
Literacy rate, 43
Live-aid rock concert, *10*

Mariam, Mengistu Haile, 32,
    36, 37
Marxist-Leninism, 2, 33, 37,
    47
Menelik II, Emperor, 27
Monarchy, 35

Moslems, 23–25, 47–48. *See
    also* Religion
Musicians, *10*, *11*

Natural resources, 18
Negus, the, 25
Nile River, 16, *17*, 18
Nixon, Richard, *30*
Nomads, 38–39, *40*

Overcultivation, 5. *See also*
    Farming
Overgrazing, 5. *See also*
    Farming
Overpopulation, 5

People, groups of, 39–41
Persecution, religious, 47
Plateau areas, 14, *15*, 16
Portugal, 24, 25

Railroads. *See* Transportation
Rainfall, 5. *See also* Drought
Red Cross, 9
Relief, 35, 55, *10*, *11*
Religion, 21–25, 47
Renaissance, Ethiopian, 24,
    50
Rock stars. *See* Musicians
Roman Catholicism, 25. *See
    also* Religion